ROANOKE COLONY

BY TERA KELLEY

Apex is distributed by North Star Editions:
sales@northstareditions.com | 888-417-0195

Produced for Apex by Red Line Editorial.

Photographs ©: Colin Waters/Alamy, cover; AP Images, 1, 16–17, 20; Science Source, 4–5, 10–11, 18–19; iStockphoto, 6, 7, 8–9, 12; Shutterstock Images, 13, 15, 22–23, 29; Theodor de Bry/John White/Library of Congress, 24; National Park Service/Wikimedia, 26; Carol M. Highsmith/Library of Congress, 27

Library of Congress Control Number: 2022911843

ISBN
978-1-63738-436-7 (hardcover)
978-1-63738-463-3 (paperback)
978-1-63738-515-9 (ebook pdf)
978-1-63738-490-9 (hosted ebook)

Printed in the United States of America
Mankato, MN
012023

NOTE TO PARENTS AND EDUCATORS

Apex books are designed to build literacy skills in striving readers. Exciting, high-interest content attracts and holds readers' attention. The text is carefully leveled to allow students to achieve success quickly. Additional features, such as bolded glossary words for difficult terms, help build comprehension.

TABLE OF CONTENTS

CHAPTER 1

THE LOST COLONY

In 1587, a group of people sailed to Roanoke Island. They wanted to start the first English colony in North America.

Roanoke Island is on the east coast of what is now North Carolina.

The group included 118 men, women, and children. John White was their leader. By winter, the group's supplies were running low. White sailed back to England to ask for help.

Sir Walter Raleigh was an English explorer. He helped pay to start Roanoke Colony.

The *Elizabeth II* is built to look like the type of ship the colonists would have used.

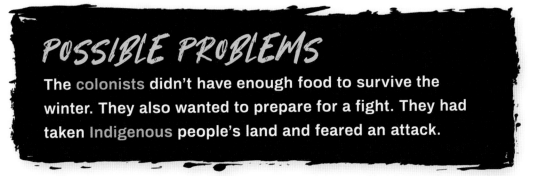

POSSIBLE PROBLEMS

The colonists didn't have enough food to survive the winter. They also wanted to prepare for a fight. They had taken Indigenous people's land and feared an attack.

Fighting between English and Spanish ships kept John White in England until 1590.

However, White got stuck in England for three years. When he returned to Roanoke, the colony was abandoned. All the **settlers** were gone.

FAST FACT

English soldiers had tried to settle on Roanoke in 1585. But they left after just one year.

CHAPTER 2

COLLECTING CLUES

White searched for clues about what happened to the colony. He found letters carved on a tree. They spelled "Croatoan."

White and his men found carvings on a tree near the colony.

Croatoan Island is now called Hatteras Island. It's about 50 miles (80 km) south of Roanoke.

Croatoan was a nearby island. White thought the settlers might have moved there. He tried sailing to it. But a storm stopped him. He had to sail back to England.

CARVING A CODE

Before White left, the settlers set up a code. If they decided to leave Roanoke Island, they would make a carving. It would tell White where they went.

The sea near Roanoke is dangerous. It often has high winds and rough waves.

White couldn't return to North America again. But other people continued the search. They looked for **evidence** of where the colonists had gone.

FAST FACT

All the houses in the colony had been taken down when White returned.

People later built a grave marker in memory of the missing colonists.

ON THIS SITE, IN JULY–AUGUST, 1585
(O. S.), COLONISTS, SENT OUT FROM ENGLAND
BY SIR WALTER RALEIGH, BUILT A FORT, CALL-
ED BY THEM
"THE NEW FORT IN VIRGINIA."
THESE COLONISTS WERE THE FIRST SET-
TLERS OF THE ENGLISH RACE IN AMERICA.
THEY RETURNED TO ENGLAND IN JULY, 1586,
WITH SIR FRANCIS DRAKE.
NEAR THIS PLACE WAS BORN, ON THE 18-
TH AUGUST, 1587,
VIRGINIA DARE,
THE FIRST CHILD OF ENGLISH PARENTS BORN
IN AMERICA—DAUGHTER OF ANANIAS DARE
AND ELEANOR WHITE, HIS WIFE, MEMBERS OF
ANOTHER BAND OF COLONISTS, SENT OUT BY
SIR WALTER RALEIGH IN 1587.
ON SUNDAY, AUGUST 20, 1587, VIR-
GINIA DARE WAS BAPTIZED. MANTEO, THE
FRIENDLY CHIEF OF THE HATTERAS INDIANS,
HAD BEEN BAPTIZED ON THE SUNDAY PRE-
CEDING. THESE BAPTISMS ARE THE FIRST
KNOWN CELEBRATIONS OF A CHRISTIAN SAC-
RAMENT IN THE TERRITORY OF THE THIR-
TEEN ORIGINAL UNITED STATES.

1896

CHAPTER 3

OTHER EVIDENCE?

In 1937, a man found a stone with a carved message. The message said the settlers had moved west. It also claimed Indigenous people had killed them.

A carved stone was found 50 miles (80 km) west of Roanoke Colony.

Researchers tried to find out if the message was real. They offered rewards for similar stones.

FAST FACT

The message claimed to be from Eleanor Dare. She was John White's daughter.

Eleanor Dare had a baby at the colony. This baby, Virginia, was the first English person born in North America.

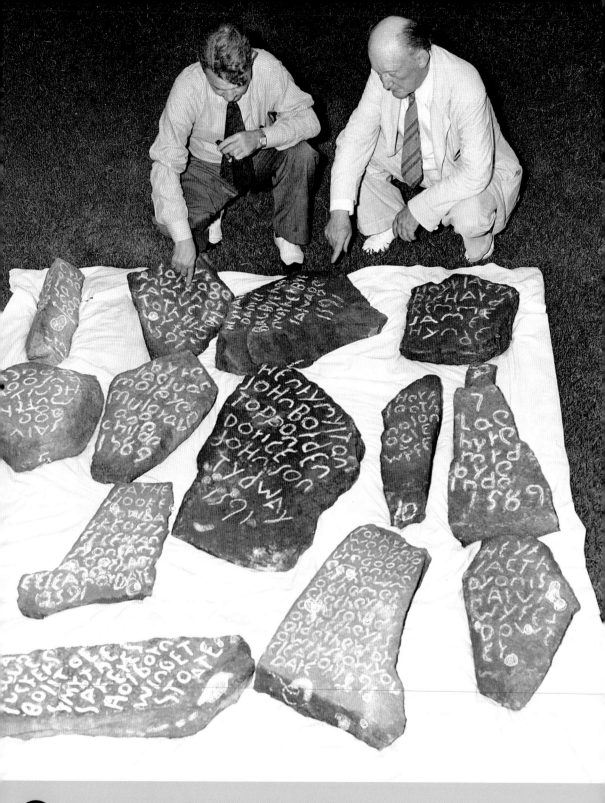

People found 47 more stones. But these were fakes. Experts found words and spelling that weren't used at the time. Many experts think the first stone was fake, too.

NOT ATTACKED

Most experts don't think Roanoke was attacked. Fights with Indigenous people did happen. But settlers often attacked first. Plus, the settlers agreed to carve a cross if they were attacked. White didn't find one.

◀ **Professors at Emory University studied the stones to test if they were real.**

CHAPTER 4

STILL UNCERTAIN

People have many theories about the lost colonists. Some believe a storm killed them. Some think they got sick. Others say they tried to sail back to England.

There are some signs colonists may have left Roanoke to move farther inland.

Many experts think the settlers went to live with Indigenous people. They may have joined local **tribes**.

TRADING PARTNERS

Settlers often lived near Indigenous people. Sometimes they traded for food and supplies. Settlers and locals could also team up to fight common enemies.

 Indigenous people had lived in the area since long before the colonists came.

Researchers dig near the colony to look for evidence.

Researchers found English **pottery** near Indigenous villages. It could be from Roanoke. Colonists could have brought it with them. But there's not enough evidence to be sure.

Today, people often visit Roanoke Island. Tours and plays help them learn about the lost colony.

FAST FACT

Some legends say the ghosts of colonists haunt Roanoke Island.

COMPREHENSION QUESTIONS

Write your answers on a separate piece of paper.

1. Write a few sentences describing the main ideas of Chapter 2.

2. Which theory about the missing colonists do you think is most likely? Why?

3. When did John White's group arrive at Roanoke Island?

- **A.** 1585
- **B.** 1587
- **C.** 1590

4. Where did John White think the missing colonists went?

- **A.** back to England
- **B.** to Croatoan
- **C.** to Indigenous villages

5. What does *survive* mean in this book?

The colonists didn't have enough food to survive the winter.

   A. to run away from

   B. to die from

   C. to live through

6. What does *abandoned* mean in this book?

When he returned to Roanoke, the colony was abandoned. All the settlers were gone.

   A. empty of people

   B. full of people

   C. full of animals

Answer key on page 32.

29

GLOSSARY

colonists
People who move to another area and take control.

colony
An area that is ruled by another country.

evidence
Information that tells what happened or if something is true.

Indigenous
Related to the original people who lived in an area.

pottery
Objects, such as bowls or vases, that are made out of clay.

settlers
People who move to a new place.

theories
Guesses about how or why something happened.

tribes
Groups of people who share a language, customs, and beliefs.

TO LEARN MORE

BOOKS

Peterson, Megan Cooley. *The Lost Roanoke Colony*. North Mankato, MN: Capstone Press, 2022.

Schuetz, Kari. *Roanoke: The Lost Colony*. Minneapolis: Bellwether Media, 2018.

Schweizer, Chris. *The Roanoke Colony: America's First Mystery*. New York: First Second, 2020.

ONLINE RESOURCES

Visit www.apexeditions.com to find links and resources related to this title.

ABOUT THE AUTHOR

Tera Kelley is the author of *Listen to the Language of the Trees*, which received a starred review from *Booklist*. She works as an editor and writer in Northern California.

INDEX

ANSWER KEY:
1. Answers will vary; 2. Answers will vary; 3. B; 4. B; 5. C; 6. A